ENCYCLOPEDIA OF RHYTHMS

Da Capo Press Music Reprint Series

ENCYCLOPEDIA OF RHYTHMS

By
JOSEPH SCHILLINGER

INSTRUMENTAL FORMS OF HARMONY

a massive collection of rhythm patterns
(evolved according to the Schillinger theory of interference)
arranged in instrumental form

DA CAPO PRESS · NEW YORK · 1976

Library of Congress Cataloging in Publication Data

Schillinger, Joseph, 1895-1943.
  Encyclopedia of rhythms.

  (Da Capo Press music reprint series)
  Reprint of the ed. published by C. Colin, New
York.
  1. Musical meter and rhythm. I. Title.
MT42.S37 1976   781.6'2   76-10326
ISBN 0-306-70782-9

This Da Capo Press edition of *Encyclopedia of Rhythms* is an unabridged
republication of the first edition published in New York in 1966.
It is reprinted with the permission of Mrs. Frances Schillinger.

workshop for pianists/guitarists/drummers/arrangers/composers

ENCYCLOPEDIA OF RHYTHMS

By JOSEPH SCHILLINGER

INSTRUMENTAL FORMS OF HARMONY

*a massive collection of rhythm patterns
(evolved according to the Schillinger
theory of interference)
arranged in instrumental form*

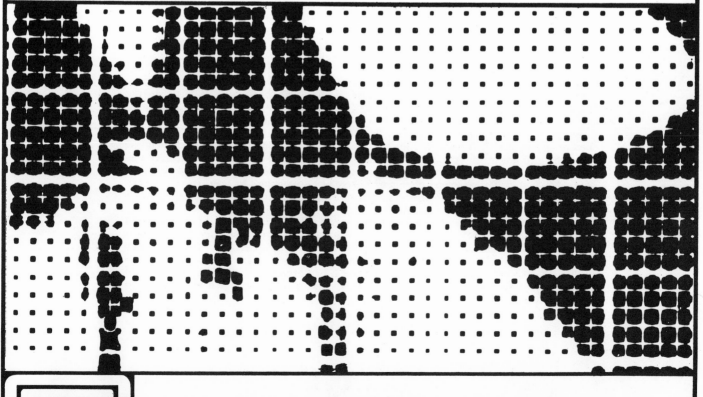

CHARLES COLIN — 315 West 53rd St., New York, N. Y. 10019

JOSEPH SCHILLINGER

Joseph Schillinger possessed one of the brilliant, analytical minds of our time. His intellect was keen enough to perceive the close relationships existing between fields that ordinarily are regarded as having little, if any, common ground. He made great advances towards convincing skeptical esthetes that science and art are not divergent, that the materials of art *include* science. The results achieved by his students, one of whom was George Gershwin, have been eloquent demonstrations of the soundness of his teachings.

Besides being a composer, conductor, and teacher of composition, Joseph Schillinger was active in visual arts and in scientific pursuits. He was born in Kharkov, Russia, in 1895. His earliest musical education was largely the result of his own experiments. In 1914 he began formal training at the St. Petersburg Conservatory. He held posts as Professor and Dean of the State Academy of Music, Ukraine (1918-22); conductor of the United Students Symphonic Orchestra, Kharkov (1918-20) and of the Ukraine Symphony Orchestra (1920-21); official of the music departments of the Ukraine and Moscow Boards of Education (1918-22); teacher of composition at the Leningrad State Institute of Musical Education (1922-28); and composer for the State Academy Theatre of Drama (1925-28); and for the State Institute of the History of Arts, Leningrad (1926-28).

In 1928, at the invitation of the American Society for Cultural Relations with Russia, Schillinger came to the United States to lecture on contemporary Russian music. He decided to settle in New York. Among his many activities were those of teacher and lecturer at the New School for Social Research, at New York University, and at Teachers College of Columbia University.

Schillinger wrote extensively on several subjects and collaborated with Leon Theremin in research in acoustics and in the design and construction of electronic instruments. In his book, "The Mathematical Basis of the Arts", he evolved a most comprehensive scientific theory of the arts, dealing with individual and compound forms based on the five senses' perception of space and time. He evolved a new system of projective geometry and, in the field of the visual arts, produced pure and industrial designs.

Schillinger's musical compositions have been performed extensively in Europe; among those which have been heard by audiences in the United States are *October*, a symphonic rhapsody with piano solo; the *First Airphonic Suite* for Theremin and orchestra; and the *North Russian Symphony* for accordion and orchestra. In addition to these compositions, Mr. Schillinger wrote other suites, some ballets and chamber music, as well as various pieces for piano and other solo instruments.

We know of many systems of music since those evolved by ancient Greek theorists, and, over the centuries, one system has replaced another. But the theories of music and the facts of the practised art have often had little in common with each other. Schillinger evolved a system by drawing on facts of the practised art of music that had previously been unexploited or unexplored. To thousands of actual works of the concededly great composers—Bach, Mozart, Beethoven, Brahms, and Wagner, among others—he applied the powerful instrument of advanced mathematical and scientific analysis. Schillinger discovered for himself that great music of all ages has been constructed according to accurate and precise principles, principles often unsuspected or unrecognized by theories of the past; he then tried to systematize his material and to evolve from it and his own imagination additional principles and new procedures.

Then came the decisive step—to determine whether these principles could be expounded in terms comprehensible to persons not trained in science and mathematics, so that such persons might successfully apply the principles in actual composition. This final step was a success. Through composers, musical directors, and conductors who were his students, Joseph Schillinger, before his death in 1943, had exerted his influence in every field of contemporary musical composition. Obviously, no musician who wishes to write in a modern idiom can afford to ignore this work.

From THE SCHILLINGER SYSTEM OF MUSICAL COMPOSITION

Published by Carl Fischer, Inc.
Reprinted by permission

A Note to the Teacher and Student

by Arnold Shaw

Co-Editor, The Schillinger System of Musical Composition
Editor, The Mathematical Basis of the Arts

It is now twenty years since THE SCHILLINGER SYSTEM OF MUSICAL COM-POSITION made its appearance in book form. For years prior to its publication, and while its originator was alive, rumors had regularly swept the academic musical community concerning the wonders of the System. Traditionalists had not been too concerned in this period over the possible challenge to their established concepts and procedures because those who studied the System with Schillinger himself were mainly musicians/ arrangers/composers in the fields of radio/recording/movies, in short, popular or utilitarian music. To be sure, the devotees were an important group of men, numbering as they did, a long list of luminaries from Glenn Miller and Benny Goodman to Oscar Levant and George Gershwin. The fact that Vernon Duke consulted with Schillinger concerning some of the serious art works he composed as Vladimir Dukelsky, was impressive. But Duke was a countryman and, despite his ballets, orchestral works and art songs, he could still be discounted as a composer of popular show music.

When the System appeared in print, however, and became accessible to all who studied or taught theory and composition, the Establishment mounted a major assault. This was both inevitable and necessary since Schillinger's work grew out of a wide - spread dissatisfaction with traditional theory and represented a revolutionary rupture with concepts that had hardened into dead-end dogmas. Of course, there had been other theorists and academicians like Hindemith and Walter Piston who had made forays on aspects of traditional theory. But they were merely trying to patch a crumbling edifice. It was Schillinger who set about erecting a completely new structure. Boldly breaking down the isolation of music theory from scientific advances, he employed concepts derived from mathematical logic, electronics and modern psychology to devise a wholly new, and workable, system of musical thought.

What was so startling about it? In pre-computer days, the use of graph paper by music students and the resort to mathematical terminology and scientific concepts became matters for criticism, if not derision. But quite recently the following appeared in *High Fidelity Magazine*: "Any existing sound or noise which can be recorded is, per se, available to the composer; a whole new set of sounds - theoretically *all* possible sounds — can be created artificially by the use of sound wave generators and other, more elaborate, electronic equipment which transfer electromagnetic impulses directly to tape; and all sounds can be manipulated, mixed and juxtaposed in virtually any possible combination." Now, there is no mention of Schillinger in the article from which this passage is quoted. But the ideas of "Music from the Electronic Universe," hardly startling today, are straight out of Schillinger. They represent a testimonial to the way that Schillinger's ideas, once treated critically if not superciliously, have today been taken up, generally without acknowledgement, by the academic community.

A

Back in the thirties, Schillinger proposed that the rule-book approach to musical theory be discarded and that the methodology of combinations and permutations be substituted. SCALES DON'T HAVE TO CONSIST JUST OF EIGHT NOTES. They can be made up of any number from 2 to 12 tones. Harmony is not a matter of consonance and dissonance but of the vertical combination of any number of tones to produce a desired sound or emotional effect. Progressions are not limited to those that have proved attractive in the past but to the mathematical number that can be devised from available resources. There was nothing sacred about symmetry and. even members; asymetrical patterns and odd-numbered formations could yield interesting music. And so it went. And so went traditional theory – down the drain.

Perhaps the most original and novel phase of Schillinger's approach was that it was the first system of musical theory based, not on harmony, but on rhythm. To be sure, he conceived of rhythm in more comprehensive terms than simply the variation of metre achieved by manipulating note durations, accents, rests and tempo. To Schillinger, while rhythm is initially a matter of note durations, it is an all-embracing concept that means PATTERN-MAKING of every conceivable type, the organization of sound in time. Not only the distribution of notes within a measure, but the arrangement of measures into groups. Not only the duration of notes within a phrase, but the length and recurrence of phrases themselves. There is also harmonic and instrumental rhythm, the former having to do with patterns of harmonic progression, the latter with the patterns of entry and exit of instruments in an orchestral work. In the present book, "instrumental forms of harmony" refers to the distribution of the segments of a chord according to a pre-developed rhythm pattern.

KEY TO MATERIAL IN BASS CLEF

The material is presented in the bass clef to emphasize that is the rhythmic basis or substructure - - the OOM-PAH, OOM-PAH so to speak - over which a melodic line can be written or superimposed. You can use it, in short, as the rhythm pattern for creating your own melodies.

Schillinger's approach to rhythm stems from the scientific theory of *interference*. Stated in mathematical terms: if two uniform, and different, periodicities overlap, or if one is superimposed on the other, a non-uniform pattern emerges, which is the fusion of the two. Without terminology: if the windshield wipers of a car are moving in identical durations, you hear a single, uniform swish-swash, swish-swash, etc.; but if one wiper is moving faster than the other, the contrasting periodicities produce an uneven pattern that may go S-W-A-S-H, swish-swish, S-W-A-S-H, etc. A similar non-uniform pattern may be produced by setting two metronomes clicking with different note values. If one metronome clicks three times in the period that the other clicks twice, the resulting sound pattern would take the following shape: C-L-I-C-K, click-click, C-L-I-C-K, etc. The relative durations would have a ratio of 2-1-1-2. In musical notation: ♩ ♪♪♩ or ♩ ♩ ♩ ♩ . The accents occur where the two metronomes click together. Enclosed within conventional bars, the first would yield a typical 6/8 pattern while the second would give us four bars of 3/4 or eight bars of 2/4. This is precisely what the student will find on page 4.

At the top of page 4, the student will also find the notation 3:2 and further down the page, 4:3. In Schillinger terminology, the colon does not represent a ratio or division relationship, but interference or synchronization. (The resultants of interference may be worked out visually, as well as aurally, through the use of graph paper, as Schillinger demonstrates in Book I of the System.) The number of rhythm patterns that may be e-volved through these procedures is virtually inexhaustible, and their variety and com-plexity are not infrequently beyond the reach of trial-and-error groping.

Once we have the resultants of interference, it is possible to augment them by splitting, or as Schillinger terms it, by *fractioning* the note durations. Beginning with page 41, this process is presented here in detail. The student will find it instructive to compare the basic patterns presented in the early pages with the more complex pat-terns presented later. For example, the one-bar pattern appearing on page 4 in 6/8 nota-tion becomes a two-bar pattern in 9/8 on page 41.

Extensive and varied though they are, the instrumental patterns presented in this book represent only a portion of the mathematically derivable resultants. For it is possible to combine three or more uniform periodicities, instead of just two. Variable velocities, or acceleration and growth series, also yield a large number of usable pat-terns. Among those that Schillinger explores in his Theory of Rhythm are the following:
1. Natural Harmonic Series: 1,2,3,4,5,6,7,8,9
2. Arithmetical Progressions: 1,3,5,7,9,11,13, etc.
3. Geometrical Progressions: 1,2,4,8,16,32, etc.
4. Power Series: 2,4,16, etc.
5. Summation Series: 1,2,3,5,8,13,21, etc.
6. Arithmetical Progressions with Variable Differences: 1,2,4,7,11,16,22,29, etc.
7. Prime Number Series: 1,2,3,5,7,11,13,19,23, etc.
These patterns may be run backwards as well as forwards and they may be developed sequentially as well as simultaneously.

Students and teachers who wish fully to understand the methodology and theory underlying the resources presented here, must turn for illumination to *The Schillinger System of Musical Composition* itself. In composition and in improvisation, there are no substitutes for judgment, taste, imagination and depth of feeling. But in order to exer-cise these faculties with discernment and impact, the performer and the composer must have as complete a knowledge as possible of the resources available to him. Earlier theorists thought of resources largely in terms of what had been successfully used. Schillinger was concerned with what had *not* been used and with making the student aware of *all* resources. Mathematics and other sciences provided the instruments for unlocking a rich storehouse of musical material that intuition by itself could only par-tially uncover. As the present work suggests, with the Schillinger System, the composer, the arranger, the performer embark on an exciting voyage of musical discovery that can only serve to enhance their creations.

C

PART I

RHYTHMIC RESULTANTS
to
INSTRUMENTAL FORMS
of
HARMONY

TABLE OF CONTENTS

D

7/8 RHYTHMIC RESULTANTS 7:5 = ♩ ♪ + ♩ + ♩. + ♩ + ♪ + ♩ ♪ + ♪ + ♩ + ♩. ♩ + ♪ ♩ 16
5 2 3 4 1 5 1 4 3 2 5

7/8 RHYTHMIC RESULTANTS 7:6 = ♩. + ♪ + ♩ ♪ + ♩ + ♩ + ♩. + ♩. + ♩ + ♩ + ♩ ♪ + ♪ + ♩. 20
6 1 5 2 4 3 3 4 2 5 1 6

8/8 RHYTHMIC RESULTANTS 8:3 = ♩. + ♩. ♩ + ♪ + ♩. + ♩. ♪ + ♩ + ♩. + ♩. 21
3 3 2 1 3 3 1 2 3 3

8/8 RHYTHMIC RESULTANTS 8:3 = ♩. + ♩. ♩ + ♪ + ♩. + ♩. ♪ + ♩ + ♩. + ♩. 22
3 3 2 1 3 3 1 2 3 3

8/8 RHYTHMIC RESULTANTS 8:5 = ♩ ♪ + ♩. + ♩ + ♩ ♪ + ♪ + ♩ ♩ + ♪ + ♩ ♪ +
5 3 2 5 1 4 4 1 5

♩ + ♩. + ♪ ♩ 22
2 3 5

8/8 RHYTHMIC RESULTANTS 8:7 = ♩ ♩. + ♪ + ♩. + ♩ + ♩ ♪ + ♩. + ♩ + ♩ + ♩. + ♪ ♩ +
7 1 6 2 5 3 4 4 3 5

♩ + ♩. + ♪ + ♩. ♩ 24
2 6 1 7

9/8 RHYTHMIC RESULTANTS 9:2 = ♩ + ♩ + ♩ + ♪ + ♪ + ♩ + ♩ + ♩ + ♩ 26
2 2 2 2 1 1 2 2 2 2

9/8 RHYTHMIC RESULTANTS 9:4 = ♩ + ♩ + ♪ + ♩. + ♩ + ♩ + ♩ + ♩. + ♪ + ♩ + ♩ 28
4 4 1 3 4 2 2 4 3 1 4 4

9/8 RHYTHMIC RESULTANTS 9:5 = ♩. ♩ + ♩ ♩. + ♪ + ♩ ♩. + ♩. + ♩ + ♩ ♩. ♪ + ♩ +
5 4 1 5 2 2 5 2

♩. + ♩. ♩ + ♪ + ♪ + ♩. ♪ + ♩ ♩. 29
3 5 1 1 4 5

9/8 RHYTHMIC RESULTANTS 9:7 = ♩. ♪ + ♩ + ♩ ♩ + ♩ + ♩. + ♩. + ♪ + ♩ ♩ + ♪ + ♩. +
7 2 5 4 3 6 1 7 1 6

♩. + ♩ + ♩ ♪ + ♩ + ♩. ♪ 34
3 4 5 2 7

9/8 RHYTHMIC RESULTANTS 9:8 = ♩. ♩ + ♪ + ♩. ♩ + ♩ + ♩. + ♩. + ♩. ♩ + ♩ ♩. +
8 1 7 2 6 3 7 4

♩. ♪ + ♩ ♩. + ♩. + ♩. + ♩ + ♪ ♩. + ♪ + ♩ ♩. 38
4 5 3 6 2 7 1 8

E

PART II

ANALYZING RHYTHMIC RESULTANTS
with
FRACTIONING

TABLE OF CONTENTS

F

7/8 RHYTHMIC RESULTANTS with FRACTIONING 7:6 = ... 116

8/8 RHYTHMIC RESULTANTS with FRACTIONING 8:3 = ... 133

8/8 RHYTHMIC RESULTANTS with FRACTIONING 8:5 = ... 142

8/8 RHYTHMIC RESULTANTS with FRACTIONING 8:7 = ... 149

9/8 RHYTHMIC RESULTANTS with FRACTIONING 9:2 = ... 162

9/8 RHYTHMIC RESULTANTS with FRACTIONING 9:4 = ... 168

9/8 RHYTHMIC RESULTANTS with FRACTIONING 9:5 = ... 178

9/8 RHYTHMIC RESULTANTS with FRACTIONING 9:7 = ... 211

9/8 RHYTHMIC RESULTANTS with FRACTIONING 9:8 = ... 232

G

PART I

RHYTHMIC RESULTANTS

to

INSTRUMENTAL FORMS

of

HARMONY

By CHARLES COLIN

These rhythmic examples are basic orchestration for a variety of musical situations. The arranger or composer needs to use each example as a catalyst and the most difficult portion of the work is completed. The most arduous part of any new composition is the actual beginning. Here Schillinger has done this for you in capsule form.

The obvious applications are:

$\frac{6}{8}$ — March, Tarantella $\frac{3}{4}$ — Waltz $\frac{2}{4}$ — March

H

12/8 RHYTHMIC RESULTANTS 4:3 =  4

For the arranger with a scientific bent the following suggestions may prove valuable. The various resultants (3:2 or 4:3) correspond to the acoustical ratios of the harmonic overtone series. This means that the rhythmic resultant of 4:3 is slightly more dissonant than the rhythmic resultant of 3:2. The former corresponds to the perfect 4th and the latter to the perfect 5th.

5/8 RHYTHMIC RESULTANTS 5:2 = ... 5

The 5/8 rhythm is traditional in many oriental cultures, e.g., Greeks, Indians.

5/8 RHYTHMIC RESULTANTS 5:3 = ... 6

Because rhythmic resultants are complete units, they are exceptionally useful at cadences, introductions, modulations, and endings.

I

5/8 RHYTHMIC RESULTANTS 5:4 =

The greater the number of times a resultant is repeated, the more is its psychological impact. This is the equivalent of playing a melodic tone louder.

6/8 RHYTHMIC RESULTANTS 6:5 =

A very good application of this example is an organ point in the lowest voice with sharply attacked chords above. This is a useful device to build up climactic tension.

7/8 RHYTHMIC RESULTANTS 7:2 =

This is commonly used in modern atonal writing. The modern composer has a wealth of ideas based on these resultants.

7/8 RHYTHMIC RESULTANTS 7:3 =  12

This can be used similarly as 7:2 except that the unit is now three measures long.

7/8 RHYTHMIC RESULTANTS 7:4 = ... 14

Whenever a rhythmic unit is changed from ♪ to ♩, the effect is to make the orchestration sound more dramatic. This can be compared to playing a melody an octave lower. Play over these examples:

16

7/8 RHYTHMIC RESULTANTS 7:5 =

A very useful rhythmic sketch for the arranger working in poly-harmony.

K

You will notice as the rhythms become more dissonant, their total durations are longer. The orchestration of a Schillinger student is thus psychologically assured.

This is another good rhythmic sketch for poly-harmony. Poly-harmony is the use of different chordal structures at different strata levels.

Schillinger's conception of Strata Harmony encompassed musical planes of melody and harmony in different registers.

L

This example can also be considered to be in $\frac{4}{4}$ or C time, another example of Schillinger's accuracy in rhythmic notation.

These examples are not meant to be static but rather dynamic, e.g.,

This is a wonderful example of an orchestral pyramid.

RHYTHMIC RESULTANTS 9:4 = ... 28

Each rhythm can be so divided so as to be applicable for florid strings, e.g.,

RHYTHMIC RESULTANTS 9:5 = 29

RHYTHMIC RESULTANTS 9:7 = 34

Students aspiring to the highest in symphonic composition should analyze this example carefully.

This example does not complete the possibilities of rhythmic examples. Rhythmic lines can interact in the same manner as chords do. Here is a rhythmic resultant of the rations: 2:3:5

PART II

ANALYZING RHYTHMIC RESULTANTS
with
FRACTIONING

By CHARLES COLIN

These rhythmic resultants, result when the smaller unit rhythm is repeated canonically.

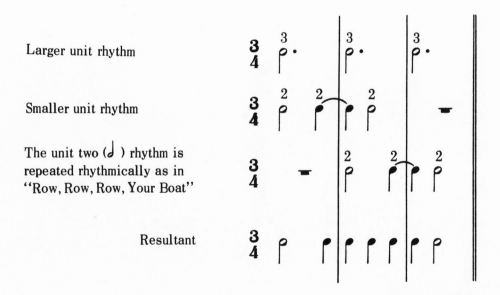

Larger unit rhythm	
Smaller unit rhythm	
The unit two (♩) rhythm is repeated rhythmically as in "Row, Row, Row, Your Boat"	
Resultant	

A Canon is when a melody is repeated exactly after a rest. It is sometimes called a "Round."

$\frac{9}{8}$ **RHYTHMIC RESULTANTS with FRACTIONING** 3:2 =

The technique of fractioning increases the possibilities for the composer. The total duration is always the larger generator squared. In this example (3^2 – 3 x 3 – 9 units) each measure is a complete resultant or nine $\frac{1}{8}$ notes.

$\frac{4}{4}\binom{16}{16}$ **RHYTHMIC RESULTANTS with FRACTIONING** 4:3 =

An easy explanation of what is meant by the interference of two or more generators is: this is the merging of two or more rhythmic patterns, so that you do not hear the original patterns but rather a new and unique pattern.

$\frac{5}{4}$ **RHYTHMIC RESULTANTS with FRACTIONING** 5:2 =

This is another useful rhythmic sketch for orchestration, demanding an oriental flavor.

Q

5/4 RHYTHMIC RESULTANTS with FRACTIONING 5:3 =  50

This example need not be used exclusively in 5/4 time. A good project is to place this resultant into a variety of meters. The results will open up new worlds for orchestration.

5/4 RHYTHMIC RESULTANTS with FRACTIONING 5:4 = 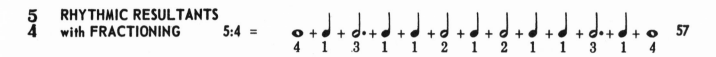 57

This example utilizing the ($\flat$ – 1) unit has a greater gestalt of excitement.

6/8 RHYTHMIC RESULTANTS with FRACTIONING 6:5 =  58

This rhythmic sketch would make a wonderful conclusion to any type of "who done it" type of program.

R

7/8 RHYTHMIC RESULTANTS with FRACTIONING

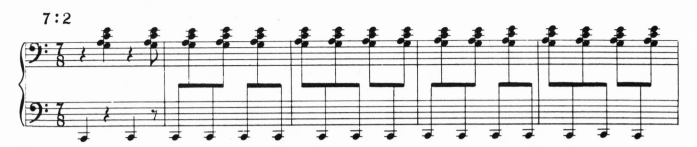

The psychological impact of this rhythm is visually obvious. With minor orchestration, a wonderful background can be written to a scene depicting an obsessive compulsive conflict.

7/8 RHYTHMIC RESULTANTS with FRACTIONING

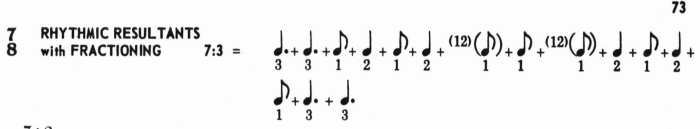

This is a good example of how to intelligently increase the rhythmic complexity or orchestration.

7/8 RHYTHMIC RESULTANTS with FRACTIONING

The constant inter-play of upper and lower voices makes this a useful device for orchestrating humor.

7/8 RHYTHMIC RESULTANTS with FRACTIONING

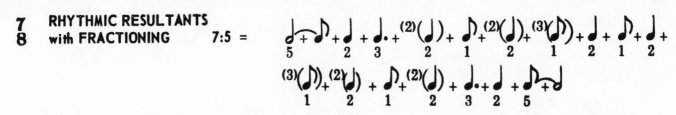

7:5 =

7:5

This is excellent for a pastoral scene. Be careful to keep the dynamic level of the upper voices at **p** and the attacks, legato.

116

7/8 RHYTHMIC RESULTANTS with FRACTIONING

7:6 =

7:6

These rhythmic sketches have immediate application for modern composers working in electronic composing devices.

133

8/8 RHYTHMIC RESULTANTS with FRACTIONING

8:3 =

8:3

The feeling of humor and excitement is obvious to the eye, in this little gem of orchestration.

T

8/8 RHYTHMIC RESULTANTS with FRACTIONING

Because resultants are symmetrical, i.e., they are the same forward and backward, they are extremely valuable for rhythmic cadences.

5 3 2 3 2 1 2 2 1 2 1 1 1   2 1 2 1 1 1 2 1 2 2 1 2 3 2 3 5

8/8 RHYTHMIC RESULTANTS with FRACTIONING

Always keep in mind that long tones may be sub-divided in a variety of ways.

9/8 RHYTHMIC RESULTANTS with FRACTIONING

162

This would make a wonderful basis for an ostinato section for a modern composition.

U

9/8 RHYTHMIC RESULTANTS with FRACTIONING 9:4

Modern arrangers and composers have a wealth of rhythmic orchestration in the Schillinger resultants. With a little experimentation this will be obvious.

9/8 RHYTHMIC RESULTANTS with FRACTIONING 9:5 = 178

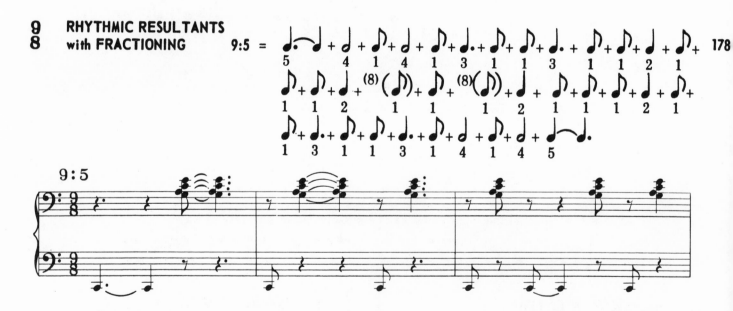

Notice the change of syncopation that occurs when this rhythm is placed in $\frac{4}{4}$ or $\frac{3}{4}$ time (where ♪ = 1).

By this time, the student is surely aware of the possibilities that can come out of these resultants. These rhythms can be used in any register and for any group of instruments.

9/8 RHYTHMIC RESULTANTS with FRACTIONING

9:8 =

232

Some of the possibilities have now been shown you. These rhythmic structures in conjunction with Schillinger's "Kaleidophone", will open up new areas of creativity until now, undreamed of.

ACKNOWLEDGEMENT

Mrs. Joseph Schillinger wishes to acknowledge the work done by Arnold Shaw and by Charles Colin. Mr. Shaw wrote the Preface, "A Note to the Teacher and Student", and Mr. Colin wrote the "Supplementary and Explanatory Key."

W

ENCYCLOPEDIA OF RHYTHM

by

JOSEPH SCHILLINGER

This is a practical handbook of rhythm patterns, one that performers, students, teach-ers, arrangers, and composers have needed for centuries. In easily usable form, it presents for the first time, the entire range of rhythm resources, making accessible to all who are interested in music the most novel, the most complex, and the most simple rhythm forms. One finds patterns that have been used again and again down the years, also hundreds that have never been used before. This is a book to be studied and treasured.

4

8

14

15

20

22

24

34

36

50

54

7:2

7:3

110

117

8:3

142

156

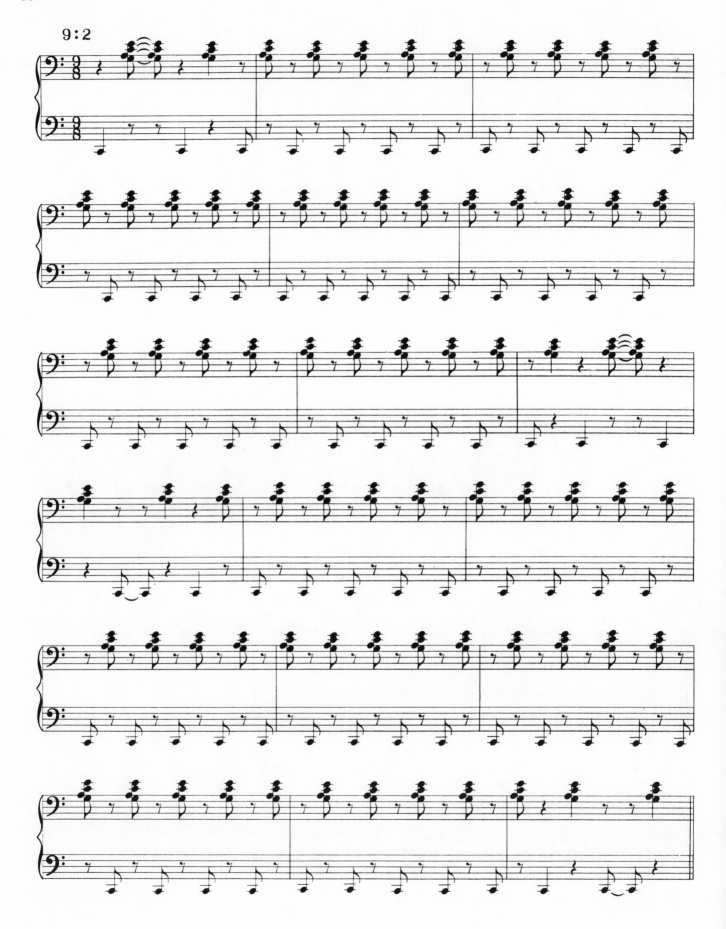

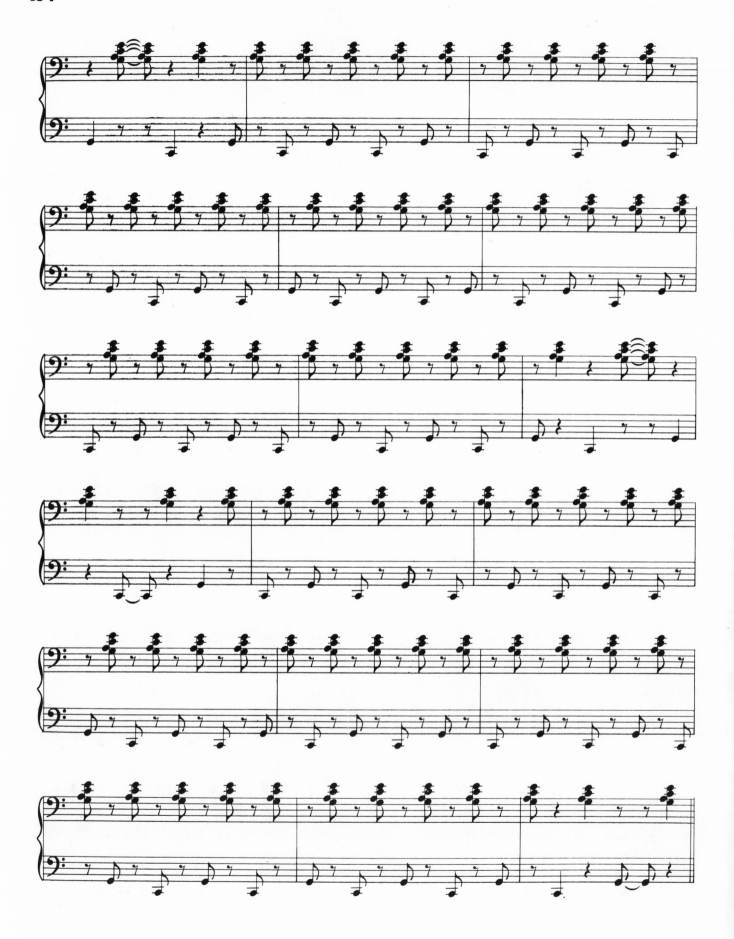

168

172

190

198

212